DEAR OSCAR

NARCISSIST IN MY BUSINESS

*"Finding the humour, lessons and blessings
within any given situation, is the difference
between us laughing or crying with tears of joy"*

#Skidangleboom

DEAR OSCAR

NARCISSIST IN MY BUSINESS

ZED REGAL

British Library Cataloguing-in-Publication Data
A catalogue record for this book is available from the British Library.

ISBN 978-1-64764-236-5

CONTENTS

ABOUT THE AUTHOR

WHAT WAS THE PURPOSE OF MY TWO-YEAR RELATIONSHIP WITH a controlling, lying, gaslighting, manipulative, demon like energy thief of a narcissist I asked myself before putting pen to paper.

I realised this experience could only come through a close relationship business venture because, there's no way I would tolerate this behaviour from anyone, male or female, in any other setting.

I thought I'd come too far within myself to become prey for any psychopath's fun and games. Though in hindsight, the lessons and blessings were all a part of my reawakening and preparation for the next part of my life's exciting journey.

The experience opened my eyes and mind to the narcissistic behaviour patterns of other people I thought I knew, and enabled me to have an even deeper understanding of the personality clashes and dynamics of my parents, which further assisted my self-healing journey.

I understood from a young age that my life experiences and how I've handled, and healed from them, are a big part of my purpose to help others to be transformed, inspired, motivated and empowered to realise, act upon and open up the abilities within them for their highest good. I've created workshops, and work one on one with clients as a Life Coach, Psychotherapist and Intuitive Holistic Healer around the best ways we can spend our T.I.M.E.

The meaning and the mindset behind the T.I.M.E acronym I created is to, Transform or be Transformed, Inspire or be inspired, Motivate or be Motivated or to be Empowered or Empower others. T.I.M.E.

So it's no surprise to me that, creatively transmuting the lessons of my experience with a narcissistic in my business, has been channelled and now manifests itself through my writing. It's a tool I often use to reveal and release any emotions and mindsets that no longer serve my highest good. As well as the personal benefits, sharing my wisdom has seemed to help so many others to accelerate their process of self-healing or inner-standing, to become stronger, or better prepared, on so many levels.

What still amazes me about this journey, is that all the videos I watched on the subject as research, didn't happen until after I had freed myself form the situation.

The information I found both highlighted, and gave me a detailed explanation for the first time ever, of how I've always carried myself as a Super Empath with a Sigma Personality type, and the best ways to handle narcissistic relationships for our protection while going through the motions.

Again, this is just another example of the purpose in all of this, my reawakening. My life experiences had prepared me for this type of abuser, and it feels like a test that I passed with flying colours.

Anyway, it's that T.I.M.E.

INTRODUCTION

"When we truly understand ourselves, we can better understand others, and assist them in their life's journey with our wisdom and experience if they want it, and more importantly, if we choose to give."

USIC IS MY FIRST LOVE. THERE CAME A TIME IN MY LIFE WHEN I'd learned, created, and was experienced in so many different areas in the creative and healing arts that, rather than running out of breath when talking about what I do, I'd simplify it to Music Media & Massage. It's within the music side of my life where I unknowingly introduced Oscar the narcissist into my business.

So that you understand where I was in my journey to greatness, I was in my third year of recovery from a life changing, leg lengthening operation. My leg had gone from being strong and thick, to resembling a matchstick as a result of the trauma my body had experienced from the operation, and I'd got to a place in my healing where I could walk but still had limiting mobility and flexibility issues.

My Harley Street doctor told me I'd be in a wheelchair before the age of forty when I was around thirteen years old. I did ev-erything in my power to both prepare for that possibility, and to prolong or avoid the prediction, while maintaining a mindset of achieving a day-to-day level of normality and balance in all areas of my life, alongside my global aspirations to realise and live out my visions and purpose.

So maintaining my physical and mental health, quickly became the foundation of everything I'd been through, and had achieved personally and professionally. And I'm still going through my healing process as I write. In fact, for the past week I've been housebound and have predominantly assumed a horizontal po-sition as a result of my muscular issues. Thankfully I've always chosen to use my down time productively, because I can't stand unnecessarily wasting time when I have creative ideas running around in my head screaming at me to express myself creatively.

Continually maximizing my time has afforded me a wealth of experience in music and the creative arts. It started from setting up my record label, where I handled everything from creating the music for multiple artists, the marketing and promotions, while organising and managing small to large music events, or cre-ative workshops to individuals or groups of people of all ages. I've performed as an Artist on some of the biggest stages in the UK, Produced and Presented popular radio shows across the south of

England, written books, and not to mention the magazine styled music related television show I created, produced and edited called Its Peak Unplugged.

I'd put in way over the generally accepted estimation of ten thousand hours to master anything, which only made Oscar's role at representing my Artist affairs even easier. Though it only seemed to trigger a variety of expressions I can only describe as jealousy and envy at this point. I'm not sharing this part of my life out of any revenge filled intentions or an ego-based mindset, it's just that sometimes, we have to celebrate ourselves and be proud to share who we are and our achievements. At least as a reminder to ourself of the journey we've overcome until the present moment, so that we can evaluate, and make a plan to action and manifest the unwritten next chapter of our life's journey.

I am an ambassador for disability in the arts, given my life's experience in that arena. I've always been selective yet open to working with, and offering opportunities to, people with

physical or psychological issues such as dyslexia and bipolar, of which Oscar had often said that he suffered from, but conveniently, only ever happened during pivotal points of conversation as a means to gain sympathy, and distract from answering direct questions.

Psychology and understanding human patterns of behaviour have always come naturally to me, which is why I studied and qualified as an NLP Practitioner, Clinical Hypnotherapist and Life Coach, to assist with my hands-on healing and talking therapy practices. In one way or another, these transferable life skills and abilities, of which I'd been practicing for years before qualifying or meeting Oscar, have become extremely useful and invaluable for me.

I say this, so that you can clearly understand the holistic approach I take when communicating with anyone about their needs in a professional, or personal setting, and the approach I naturally take within any working relationship I'm involved with, while finding the best solutions to have a balanced, and harmonious experience for all involved.

I've always found that clear communication, with understanding in all directions when working in a team, are a top priority for me. Attempting to empower yourself with information, that could possibly work against a narcissist's intentions, are a big red flag for the Oscars of this world lurking around one's business, trying to covertly orchestrate mayhem while thinking they're being clever.

If there's one thing that I've learned from my experiences is that, without a balanced mental and, in my case the additional, physical wellbeing, even one imbalance or limitation can affect every area of our life if we let it, and are not proactive towards growth, change, and transformation within ourselves. How we think eventually manifests in to our daily reality, negatively or positively.

Introducing Oscar into my life affected both of these areas in its peak of the unknown Oscarprickisms, for many reasons I now see with more clarity as his attempts, some being successful, to control me and infiltrate my business affairs as a means to steal, cheat and lie behind my back for his own greedy intentions.

The quote at the start of this chapter has been a key motivator in my pursuit of happiness, financial and creative freedom and overall independence. Fused with love and empathy, I've found it to be an invaluable mindset tool that has helped to protect me, and project my energies accordingly when required.

This is a valuable tool we can all adopt when dealing with a narcissist in your life and business.

CHAPTER ONE
THE POWER OF HUMOUR

"I laughed so hard that I passed wind and called it an Oscarfart. Gas and waste removal".

So, I gave Oscar the opportunity to play a manager's role within my music and entertainment business.

I am the CEO of my label Catchy Creation, and I'm signed as a singer/songwriter and performing artist to my label. It should go without saying that I've opted for the best contractual conditions possible for my music, and protection of my image and interests as an artist, while aligning with the best interests of the labels objectives and grand vision, for an infinite period of time.

I'll get into some of the various conflicting scenarios that inspired my writing throughout this book, though one thing that helped me through this journey was humour.

You have to 'Play fool fi ketch wise' is a Jamaican saying I've heard throughout my life. The English equivalent could be translated as – 'say less, watch and listen more to see through their bollocks!

Recognising the repeated and unnecessary lies, and attempts to deceive became amusing to me, because it served as motivation to finding humorous and creative ways of protecting my energy, while still moving forward with what I knew to be part of the divine plan for me and my journey.

So I changed his name to Oscar. Oscar Oscarprick.

Meaning the level and depth of acting, which was bad acting once I'd recognised it may I add, and the skills and abilities he used to deceive and manipulate me, and others in relation to me and my business, became laughable. So, I gave him the soon to be world famous, Oscarprick award.

I'm bussing up laughing right now as I say his name aloud. Actually, when I first heard his full name, my initial feeling was that it sounded made-up, like a child had created it. Sincere apologies to the Oscarprick family if my thought was inaccurate on his inherited last name. But his new name brings more joyful vibrations to the world in my opinion.

I mean, I've come across some people with effed up names in my time, so I'm always open-minded and respectful whenever this has been my experience, though Oscar Oscarprick seems like such a fitting name for the person I overcame and endured for 2 years of my life.

Anyway, this is a tool I eventually used to positively and immediately affect my mood whenever I had to communicate with Oscar through technology.

Rather than feeling pissed off or drained at the mere thought or sight of having to engage in another conflicting conversation with Oscar, seeing their new name had me laughing in stitches before every encounter.

It programmed my mind so well that I had to make a conscious effort not to let the name slip when around people, in a business setting, or when talking directly to Oscarprick.

This is just one of the fun and creative things you can do to protect, transform, and empower yourself, before having to interact with your version of Oscar within your business or life.

* *Use humour to lighten your mood.*

My ability to reflect and transform negative energy directed at me, to something useful, has been a skill I was instinctively forced to learn as a child through the emotionally abusive relationships absorbed through my parents.

Oscar's ability to build rapport with people using humour, talk that attempts to put you on a pedestal, and acts of kindness can rank high among the best of most socially active individuals. Though it's the mindset and intention to be controlling and deceptive in a calculated way that we need to be aware of.

The mind games that Oscar like to play are designed to negatively affect your mindset based on your response to their actions or inactions.

Hopefully, you know yourself well enough to know when someone isn't being straight with you. If you're still evolving and not fully at that stage yet, I pray that my journey assists your T.I.M.E to not allow the Oscarpricks of this world to program your actions, or your patterns of thinking.

Understanding how to program yourself, at least, to protect your mind state where possible when managing a relationship with Oscar, is one of the best things you can learn and implement.

CHAPTER TWO
ENERGY PROTECTION TOOL

"Understanding something or someone empowers us to make better decisions for our highest good."

I'M THINKING HOW I CAN BEST DESCRIBE WHAT I INSTINCTIVELY done with my energy in order to manage myself, and tolerate the narcissistic abuse from Oscar for so long.

Imagine you're at the centre of an energetic ball of light around your body that stretches ten miles.

There are ten evenly placed circles that get smaller the closer it gets to your body, and you are positioned in the last and smallest circle in the centre. This section is zero miles.

Every time I understood a negative pattern of behaviour and conduct from Oscar, or he'd piss me off to the point of evaluating whether or not to get rid of him, I'd bring my energy protection ball of light, aka boundaries, back towards me one mile at a time.

A one-mile countdown from ten to zero. Zero represents the place of having no energetic space for Oscar's antics, only what was best for my highest good while continuing to make progress with my goals for my music, brands and businesses.

Which, may I add, is also the place of giving almost zero fucks about showing understanding, empathy, love and openness through any means of communication in regards to moving forward in business with Oscarprick.

Now I know it may seem that I say the name Oscar a lot, and that's mainly to help replace any potential sting you may feel triggered, with humour, when relating my journey to your own experiences with an Oscarprick, who could be male, female, or anything they might identify as.

I just followed a trail of thought while writing and google searched for personal descriptions of Oscar, here's what came up.

- Egomaniac,
- The devil's child – hence the childish and petty behaviours.
- That prick!

I know I'm digressing from the point I'm trying to make, though if you could witness the deep belly laughter and natural spring water dribbling down my face after spurting it out uncontrollably upon coming across the "that prick!" quote on my second computer screen, you'd understand. (Thought to self – If I put laughter emojis here, it would probably fill up the rest of the page).

Anyway. Point zero is the place of keeping everything close to my chest. I was fully prepared and armed to take my exit from this toxic working relationship. I had a long list of mental notes and audio recordings of red flag moments should I need to prove my experience to anyone.

This experience included gaslighting, aggressive and abusive conduct, the constant lies and attempts at fear tactics and mental manipulations, the unbelievably stupid, devilish and unprofessional actions Oscar would choose to take with collaborating creatives and professionals while trying to contain and covertly control everything. Sound familiar?

Fortunately for me, every time I reduced my protection circle a mile, aka limited the energy I allowed in to my space or project out towards Oscar, this process empowered me. It helped me regain a sense of control over certain areas within my business affairs with him.

My decision to refocus my energy toward myself triggered Oscarprick. He'd often try and lash out with a partially concealed venomous tone of voice full of insults that supposedly came from someone else and not him, to which I'd put him straight at first. Because I chose to 'play fool fi ketch wise', his repeated patterns of ever deepening levels of applaudable acting and fabricated stories to regain control of a given situation became even more comical. The consistent pattern of talking or acting out in ways to provoke a reaction, any reaction, as fuel to create and sustain conflict were his attempts to distract and control.

Combined with his sketchy responses or lack of response to most communications, along with a dose of business-related frustrations, I continued to lean on humour for support.

So, I mirrored Oscar and played him at his own game for a short period as an experiment to test my theories about him, on him, for my own real-life confirmation. Seeing his frustrated reactions, and stuttering nonsense of randomly weaved words to wriggle his way out of being honest, did make me smirk on occasion, given the Oscarprickisms he'd often covertly display privately and within group settings.

I saw it as an interestingly amusing, short-lived, psychopath in my business, social experiment.

My life's adventures have taught me that, if I have to stoop to someone's level in order to feel empowered or like I've achieved anything of true value, it will only lower my vibration and limit the true level of what can be achieved. If we can manage ourselves accordingly and endure the challenge to rise through and above it, the results will deliver a wiser and stronger version of ourself ready for the next chapter of our life.

So in summary, it's a powerful self-help tool for putting emotional and mental boundaries in place, thus protecting your energy.

The closer you bring your circle of light energy to your centre, the more clarity of mind and control you have over your abilities to navigate the Oscarprickarious challenges we may face.

Make sense?... Good.

CHAPTER THREE

FAMILIARITY

"Have you ever looked at someone and thought... DICKHEAD?"

M Y CORE PERSONALITY TYPE IS A SIGMA FUSED WITH THE ATTRI-butes of a Super Empath. I've only recently found this information out as a result of the recent experience I've endured and overcome. As I learned about personality types, I found that everything I came across talking about sigma males, amazingly detailed with exact precision how I've always carried myself, and my mindset, for as long as I can remember.

So, my ability to spot, tolerate and handle any form of bollocks and shady behaviours and energies from people is at hybrid levels. I've always known it. Though it was a joy to see it reaffirmed, and that there is a term that describes people like me. Thanks YouTube content creators.

This new found understanding highlighted to me how I managed to be around that dickhead Oscar for so long and remain calm, composed and purposeful throughout the narc abuse storms, and still have enough energy to show empathy, understanding and compromise, within reason, for the highest good in any given moment. Sometimes we have to try new ways of operating within business to evaluate if the change is positive or not. If not, and the tried and tested way wasn't broken, it will suffice until a better strategy is implemented. At least, that's my mindset in relevant situations.

Within the first six months of building a relationship with Oscar, I'd mentally noted more 'amber flags' than I have toes and fingers in relation to his character. Though, through some his actions, I could also see some of the necessary and potentially valuable traits of a grafter, of which I'd expect to see from anyone who professes to be the best manager in the world. The positive situations are what made me cautious but confident to continue to work with him.

Though let me give you some examples of the 'amber flag' Oscarprickarious actions that alerted my 'proceed with caution' senses.

As we do when getting to know someone who we'll potentially have a long-term working relationship with, you ask relevant questions. One of the first question I asked was, who have you managed? Until this very day, he still hasn't answered that question! The only thing he's said, about a year after me repeatedly asking is, that he could've managed Amy Winehouse if she didn't pass away. That was the only name he mentioned. Dickhead.

The very first person I put Oscar in contact with to speak on my behalf was someone I didn't want to work with. Oscar often talked of being a great negotiator in import meetings from his past experiences in the music industry, and often made a point of highlighting that as manager, his role was to take the weight off of the Artist so that I can focus on creativity, which is right. Within minutes of me giving him the first task of making a phone call, the contact immediately rang me to warn me about Oscar, saying that he's greedy and only in this for the money. He also wished me good luck before we concluded the call. I mentally noted the amber flag. Then, I questioned Oscar about it, to which he had a plausible story, of which I didn't really care to question deeper.

Oscar seemed to be showing some leadership qualities while organising, and physically working on bringing a music venue to life. During one of our conversations in the venue, I'd told him a snippet of what my plans were for the continuation, of a segment, of my music television show. Days later, he proposed an idea to me that was the exact same thing I'd told him about, just with a different name! It's safe to say from this point onwards, I kept any ideas and plans that wasn't relevant to our relationship to myself. He tried to steal my idea! Dickhead.

When everything went sour between Oscar and the venues owners, he'd talk to me about his plans to rob the venue. Yes, I said break in with the set of keys he still had and remove their expensive electrical equipment without consent as revenge for their breakdown in communication.

He spoke it in a way that felt like he was trying to coerce me into joining in with his hype and offer to assist him. Of course, I didn't.

I was fifteen years old the last time I stole anything, so why would I even think about doing anything like that now? And more importantly, you're even older than I am! Now I'm left questioning and monitoring the mindset of this dickhead.

I simply said to him, "let me know how it goes", and made another red flag mental note instead of getting rid of him there and then because, he wasn't planning on stealing from me. Was he?

> *"People may not always tell you who they are,*
> *But they will always show you."*

Because my energy was open, and my mindset was in a place of helping Oscar integrate, and fully understand my Artist, and Business objectives so he could maintain the high standards I'd set for my business, we'd have many discussions that would often become conversations sprinkled with low level conflict.

At first, I simply looked at it as learning to understand a new person I'm working with, in order to achieve the optimal, and reciprocal communication possible, for the highest good of moving towards our goals.

All that was really happening from Oscarpricks point of view, was that I was giving him ammunition or fuel, further enabling him to, overexaggerate his repeated patterns of talk in an attempt to program my mind, disguised as motivation. On one side of the coin, this was a good thing, but on the other side, I could clearly feel the falseness of his actions and continued to make mental notes.

Randomly nit-picking at minor or irrelevant things, and turning them into long and unnecessary conversations that drained your energy and mood by the end of it, was a common occurrence. He'd also act like he didn't understand something, keep repeating the same mistakes and act the fool while negatively reacting to my constructive criticisms, using deflective techniques to confuse and make everything sound like I was the person at fault. Dickhead.

While I was becoming very comfortable in my abilities to deal with the many quirks, and annoying nuances of what I thought was Oscars Dyslexia or Bi Polar kicking in, I became very familiar with his patterns of behaviour and character traits.

And while Oscar was getting comfortable playing gaslighting games and subtle manipulations, feeling like it was all going unnoticed, he was getting familiar with the patterns of behaviour I allowed him to see. This always kept me at least 4 steps ahead energetically and physically, despite getting to a point where I felt, and actually said it to him in person if I recal, that I felt like I didn't have any control.

I can imagine him driving home in his car after that encounter, laughing at the conversation, thinking that he'd got me exactly where he wanted me to be. Controlled. Because I instinctively kept my valuable cards close to my chest as a result of his covert conduct, Oscarprick had no idea about the depth of spiritual insights I'm blessed with, or that he'd entangled himself with his arch nemeses as a narcissist, which is a Super Empath. You dickhead.

I guess the key take away from this, is that there is no way to tell if we are in a relationship with an Oscar at first.

We just have to pay close attention to the words, actions, and energies of people surrounding us, so that we can better protect ourself from the abuse.

Whether we are strong minded or otherwise, the narcissist will view any and all of our responses to their fun and games as fuel, whether it's a positive or negative response, to continue to manipulate and control situations in their favour.

So, if you are in a relationship with an Oscar in your business or personal life, here's a few tips:

- Protect your energy
- Say less, listen more. Be mindful of how much information you give of yourself, no matter how alluring or charming, humorous or familiar they may come across as
- Trust the signs and your instincts. If your instincts are seemingly asleep, just remember the flaky conduct you've observed or heard, and the red flag mental notes taken.

And finally, in order to help bring additional light and humour to your Oscarprick encounters, don't forget to say the magical word of the day out aloud or silently, (because it can be a great stress reliever) ... YOU DICKHEAD!

CHAPTER FOUR
THE WONKY WEB WEAVER

*"Manipulation is when they blame you
for your reaction to their disrespect"*

CAN'T STAND TWO-FACED PEOPLE. THEY'LL SMILE AND SAY ONE thing to your face, then stab you in the back by trash talking your name. In Oscarpricks case, he'd say one thing to your face, and then have the audacity to say something different in the following conversation, which could be seventy-two minutes later, and make out that he didn't say that! Oi dickhead, are you mad?

Actually, that was an attempt to psychologically manipulate his way into my head so that I'd begin to second guess myself. There isn't one documented case of Alzheimer's in my family, and any possibility of short-term memory loss from a nice piece of Jamaican high-grade went out of the window the first time I recognised your shady behaviour.

If you're someone who claims to be the best music manager in the world, or the best anything (and no, not the best Oscarprick), trying to cause confusion within the Artist one is supposed to be managing, by creating layers of ego-based and self-centred control tactics, is not the best way to prove to the company you're commissioned by, that you're worthy.

At first, because I had experienced helping people with bi-polar in various personal and professional settings, I didn't really look at Oscar's over exaggerated talk and actions as a personality disorder outside of the understanding I had acquired over time about the condition. As I write and reflect on our conversations, I'm now very sceptical that his Bi-Polar was actually a real thing. It could've just been a cover story for being a hybrid narcissist. I wouldn't put it past him because it's what Oscarpricks do. They create a web of words strung together with lies for their own hidden agenda.

I've come across all kinds of manipulators in my life, so I know too well how to handle or distance myself accordingly, and still function at one hundred percent, regardless of any negative energies directed my way.

We've all come across the instigator type at some point. You know the ones who likes to mischievously stir up trouble in a playful way. Though it's a different end of the spectrum when it's constantly done in a way that provokes internal or external conflict. Having to regularly deal with that type of shit could have anyone feeling exhausted and drained, similar to how being in a relationship with someone who's never wrong could affect you. You know that person who will clearly be in the wrong, and argue a point until they're blue in the face leaving everyone feeling exhausted at the palava, rather than take accountability and fix their ways so everything can move forward in harmony.

We can never really tell what end of the Oscarprick spectrum we're dealing with, without time and connection. It can take time for you to figure out the pattern of offending behaviours, or the true source of your patterns of stress, especially if you've got an Oscar entangled in your business affairs, trying to use calculated false displays of support and helpfulness, like using money or a, 'look what I've done for you' attitude, to validate their false sense of entitlement, to control what isn't there's to control.

I didn't blaze my trail through the treacherous jungles of life without gaining valuable experiences, and life lessons for my specific purpose and destiny, without coming across a fair few one-uppers either. You know that person who just can't seem to let others shine. They always have to find a way to outdo someone, or be the best at everything, and will resort to lies to do so. If you've got twenty quid in your pocket, they've got twenty-two quid and twenty-two pence. If you climbed Mount Everest, they've climbed Mount Everest twice in one day just for a warm up session before going to have sex. The reality in my story was, that Oscar hadn't had not even a sniff at human genitalia in the whole time of knowing him.

I kinda feel like I'm ranting a little bit, though my intention is only to highlight some of the things I've experienced, so that you can be aware and better prepared to detect a potential Oscar in your life.

Rant continued.

Dickhead Oscar Oscarprick, is one of those people who may, constantly try and talk over you in a conversation to exert their illogical opinions on you, be totally dismisive, and try to confuse or reframe the conversation to fit his agenda. It's worse when they do it to try and look superior in front of others, and especially at the expense of others, which usually plays out as someone unknowingly being used, or stepped on, in order to get what Oscar wants. By any negative means necessary.

The first few times I witnessed what I perceived to be Oscars' go getter approach to some things, I took it as one of the qualities required for a manager's role. Coming across someone who could potentially attract new opportunities, and handle any global networking required, alongside myself as the CEO of my label should it be necessary, at that stage in my life, I thought he could be an asset.

Learning and understanding over time that Oscar was a liability, things had got to a place of, constantly having to second guess his true intentions when dealing with him in person, or when he had to communicate with other people on my behalf.

Introducing Oscar to some of the contacts I'd acquired, through good working relationships over the years, could've been jeopardised. They'd ring me almost immediately after talking with Oscar, querying his shady conduct, and their feelings of being spun an exaggerated, fabricated jackanory story.

Protecting the integrity of my business and my mindset, was key to ensuring this experience didn't become a waste of my time and energy.

Because Oscar outwardly voiced noticing my energy shift, often whinging that I was being cold or keeping secrets from him (blah blah blah), he would resort to sly criticisms sprinkled within almost every communication, of which I'd ignore or creatively deflect, with a mindset of maintaining the bigger picture goals to achieving the best possible outcome.

This type of relationship can easily go undetected by onlookers, or working partners with an Oscarprick in a position to influence the narrative.

Whether you're isolated while caught in an Oscar web and it happens secretly, or it happens through covert manipulation of false pieces of information, which are concocted to program others to have a negative impression of the person being – knowing or unknowingly - abused by Oscar, this can become a serious challenge. Especially if you're that someone who's unable to express or talk about it with someone else, for whatever reason, for your own peace of mind.

Oscar trying to control an entrepreneur like me, a Super Sigma Empath, to fit his own agenda, is like putting a pride of wild lions in a cage made of candyfloss as an attempt to imprison. At least, that's how it feels as I reflect on my instinctual actions taken to handle his web of lies and deceit.

There are plenty of well-intended and honourable reasons why someone would need to weave a web within business affairs. Though it is not a smart move to weave wonky webs. That's an Oscarprick move.

CHAPTER FIVE

MENACE TO SOCIETY

"Whose responsibility is it to help empower others to better protect their energy and their livelihood?"

A s I THINK OF ALL THE PEOPLE WHO HAVE BEEN INTRODUCED TO this part of my journey through Oscar, I see a clear pattern. Everyone seemed to mysteriously disappear after a short period of time, for either similar health reasons or because of something I had supposedly said. Considering Oscar was the only person communicating with them, away from the odd group chat or three-way conversations that, essentially enabled him to monitor all talk so he could control the narrative, it's hard to fathom how it could possibly be my fault.

In reality, they were all exhausted from the excessive long voice notes on WhatsApp, and the constant pestering calls demanding their time, and energy, with no regards for their busy life schedules. Any successfully connected calls, (And I say this because many quickly started to distance themselves from him), would've been purposely stretched out by Oscar for hours if allowed, in the vein of building rapport, whereas the majority of correspondence could easily have been concluded in a lot less time. This is much closer to the real reason for their departure.

So, for all the people that had to endure any form of unnecessary and stressful communications with Oscar while he was representing my music interests, I apologise. Hopefully, you've evolved as a result of your experience like I have, and I wish you the best.

As I think of all the people he's already connected with, and those who are about to fall prey to an Oscarprick attack on the senses', it fills my fingers with an increased word per minute speed and a feeling of urgency to share my story.

You won't recognise this predator at first, because Oscar will come disguised as someone who's charming or funny, shows a seemingly genuine interest in you and comes across as someone who's empathic, and is willing to help out in any way possible.

He could be that random stranger who uses a DSLR camera and a massive accessory rucksack as a tool to outwardly look professional and trustworthy, as a means to engage in seemingly random conversation. In reality, Oscar is out on the hunt for new souls to feed his uncontrollable appetite for Oscarprickisms caused by his mental disorder.

Somebody get this guy a woman. Actually no, don't. I can clearly understand why most woman wouldn't want to be with an

Oscarprick long-term, after experiencing some of his sketchy ass mannerisms. His double standards, and inability to clearly and honestly communicate with anyone concerning my business, required an Oscar award for the audaciously careless, and improper conduct I witnessed, and had received concerning phones calls about.

I have a deeply spiritually connected friend who would often run joke with me and say "Regal, don't clart the help". Meaning, don't mix business with pleasure, which is a widely accepted rule I've always understood and adhered to. Well at least ninety percent of the time, if I reflect on my journey over the previous twenty years.

Oscar would occasionally talk about the importance of not mixing business with pleasure during our conversations about the adventure that lay ahead. So I was shocked to learn that, he'd been sexually harassing a collaborator who was brought in to handle a few clerical bits for him. She was in a relationship, and had clearly expressed her disinterest in him so often, that she had to get her friend, who was working with Oscar and the person that had introduced them, to have a word to get him to back off!

As with everything else, a pattern of behaviour became more apparent the more he was around women. Like talking uninvited crud on the phone to a Jamaican dancer he met on the day I was performing at Notting Hill Carnival, to his unprofessional conduct while filming women at public and private events. I even had a promoter call me with talk about his mannerisms, out of respect for the good working relationship we'd built over time.

The deeper I studied this pretender, the more his shady talk and actions invoked a feeling inside of me, that he was possibly on a sex register somewhere under his real name before changing it by deed poll to Oscar Oscarprick.

I'd known him for two years and didn't know when his birthday was, which I thought was odd considering this was a working relationship with the potential to grow over the years, for the right person of course. I found it strange that, he never wanted pictures to be taken with him in it, and the fact I had nothing to verify anything he'd spouted about doing in his past, via anyone or anything, were additional red flag moments.

I did try to confirm my suspicions, however my attempt was unsuccessful. Requesting an enhanced DBS check was the only option remaining. I knew that I'd face fierce opposition and lack of trust accusations at the request, and I was already in a place of knowing Oscar's character had no resemblance to the team of professionals or creatives I'd been actively manifesting over the years, in any capacity, so I swiftly moved on.

Not everyone is an Oscarprick. Though it's important that we are alert to the small signs and signals, and not dismiss the intuitive gut feelings we have about people or situations. Those gut feelings are the very thing that have saved my life or my sanity on many occasions. It guides us, and protects us throughout our life journey, no matter if our decisions lead to favourable or unfavourable outcomes at first sight.

I've lost count of the challenging life circumstances I was blessed with from an early age. Coming from a home that excelled in abuse over love, to living with and manging a physical disability, one of the most valuable insights I've overstood, through recognising the life patterns that don't serve my highest good, and adjusting my pattern of thoughts, and actions to better align them with who I am becoming, is that, everything that has happened for me, is a divinely orchestrated experience designed to help prepare me, for whatever my purpose is in this life.

"There are always good things that can come out of bad situations, if you are open minded enough to see the blessings within the lessons or stresses."

CHAPTER SIX
THE LAYERS ARE DEEP

*"I don't wanna waste no time with negative
vibes, that could leave me screwing"*

COINCIDENTALLY, ALL OF THE MUSIC I'VE WRITTEN AND RELEASED
in the last year have all been around the topic of transforming
the negative energies of people around me, or brought around me
while working with Oscar, to something positive for me. Using
the creative arts for self-expression while conveying stories that
inspire and uplift could be one example, or the book you're reading
right now.

I've come to a realisation that, three of my songs titled Suh Di
Ting Guh, Pose Like and Can't Stop Me Now, all take you on a
start-middle-end journey of the relationship I had with Oscar.
I'm like a creative sponge that soaks up everything around me,

recycling energy to deliver works with truth and substance that convey messages of love while connecting with my fans. It's funny listening to them now, because when I was writing them, I wasn't actually writing about Oscar. I was inspired by his actions, and fused it with other life experiences and mindsets, to deliver a timeless piece of music. All I hear now, is me talking about the narcissistic experience I was going through, while offering mindset hacks on how I managed an Oscarprick in my business.

As I give myself closure on this part of my life, every word of my songs seems so relevant in aiding my clear inner-standing of the reasons, and purpose of our relationship.

Oscar would always try to program me by saying things like, "You're just an Artist - let me handle everything", or always act like he was better than me as a reaction to me constantly having to pull him up on various things, so that he could learn to align with the standard of services I required. So when I got the universal download for how the Pose Like video was to be filmed and delivered, I quickly started to plan every last detail.

Ensuring that everyone involved is well informed and happy with operations has always been a priority for me in any collaborative project I've headed. I used my experience in media & television production to give clear filming and edit directions to the videographer, while taking precautions to limit all communications with Oscarprick and the main people involved with the shoot. This was to ensure a stress-free experience was achieved by everyone. It was also a priority for completing the task at hand within three weeks, without any of the anticipated Oscarprick dramas I instinctively knew would arise, should I allow him too much of an active role.

His only role was to part finance the video, buy a few clip boards for the video release forms I'd prepared for the supporting artists, and ensure the needs were met of everyone in attendance, according to the plans I had set.

Long story short. There were a few improvisations on the day, of which the planning had taken into account, but everything went as smoothly as possible. Happy days.

It was months after the event that I was to learn that, the only person who had any communication with Oscar about attending the video shoot, had complaints about me, and the execution of the production not taking them into account, over concerns of not being fed.

Considering I had meticulously planned and group emailed everybody concerned with the relevant details for the days shoot, including the food and drink, of which I personally prepared and organised for everyone schedule to attend, and repeatedly explained everything to Oscar so that he understood, and could easily articulate the plan of action to the few people he may need to communicate with, I was surprised but not surprised at hearing the complaint.

When you have someone who pretends to listen, then decides to go against the plan for reasons of self-importance, and perceived control and power to those outside of the working circle, that's always going to be an issue. And it's a common documented trait found in the many people with narcissistic personality disorder (NPD).

This is just an example of how I had to protect my energy and business while still functioning professionally and accordingly, while leading my team as the producer, director and lead role to a successful conclusion.

"From you see them you will know them..." is a line from one of my favourite Reggae Artists, Capleton. This sentence just reinforces the notion that, when we have understanding of ourselves, we can better understand others.

If we can recognise and be aware of the subtle signs that alert us of danger, to our peace of mind or anything, then we are better prepared to handle the harsh realities that can plague many of us daily, through the Oscarpricks in this world or any other life challenges we may face.

CHAPTER SEVEN
SCREAMING WITH RAGE

*"Breathe deeply in through the nose,
and out through the mouth.
Now say it out loud... I'm done"*

WHEN YOU WITNESS A WOMAN SCREAMING WITH RAGE IN A professional setting, two different women, with so much anger that one storms off of the video set during production, and the other at the end of production, something is seriously wrong.

Terrible communication skills, misleading promises to get actors to attend a weekend location shoot, and continued condescending comments throughout the duration of filming directed at the actors, along with overbearing and over controlling actions, was what Oscarprick brought to the second video shoot. I mean, how can you promise three actors that you'll provide accommodation, namely erecting two tents and inflatable mattresses and food, and then only provide a sleeping bag and no food on the first day. These actors had to sleep in the back of a car with the seats down instead of what they were promised.

Don't get this twisted. Any dramas weren't down to the director, who was focused on directing a team of creatives when everything was going on, neither was it down to me, who had nothing to do with any of the organising, except for buying some of the props, and my clothing for the shoot. I was there with a role to play, as the lead actor for the two videos that were planned, just like everybody else.

Oscar had a thing for putting people on a pedestal that he considered to be important, and got caught up in sucking the dry bogies out of the arsehole of a cool and calm natured professional I'd introduced him to. Because this man happened to be a highly accomplished and respected film director, Oscar started acting over arrogantly and paraded around with an energy of I'm mister big bollocks coz I'm working with Bushy (Bushy being the pseudonym I'll use here for the sake of not disclosing his real name). Bushy was writing the script and organising cameras and crew, though because he was committed to another job in the crucial week of planning our video, Oscar was appointed as the point of contact when Bushy was unavailable, leaving him responsible for orchestrating parts of the production planning.

With his overinflated feeling of importance, I could see from his energy and actions that this was his attempt to compete with me, after the success of the Pose Like video I'd directed previously. This Oscarprickarious behaviour progressed to him not communicating with me, either as the Artist he was supposed to be managing, or as one of the actors that he was temporarily appointed to communicate with.

I reached out to Oscar for the addresses of the locations we were filming at, with no reply. After receiving the address elsewhere, I turned up to the first location, and naturally exchanged pleasantries as one would expect when working with a new team of people. Oscar wasn't there when I arrived. I was stood in front of the locations entrance, by the roads edge when I saw him walking up the road toward the venue. He looked me straight in my face, and blanked me as he continued to walk past me, which was only about a meter or two away from where I was stood. Didn't say a word. He kept this behaviour up for the whole weekend, except for when he'd randomly shove his DSLR camera in my face and say "say something!"

Given that situation, what would you do?

I chose to protect my mind state by closing my energy off to Oscar and mirroring his silent treatment, unless it was absolutely necessary for us to speak. My communication and hands-on assistance were great with everyone else on set. Though I'd spend most of the time in solitude, led on the grass mediating or giving myself a Reiki healing in the warm sun while waiting to get ready for my scenes. Keeping my mind focused on what I was there to do, deliver a convincing on-screen performance, was my objective because the show must go on. And I wasn't going to allow any Oscarprickisms to affect my mind state. If I didn't conduct myself in a calm and collected way, for the highest good of everything we were to accomplish as a team by the end of the weekend, the final product could've been negatively affected, as a result of the control issues and manipulative mind games in constant play from Oscar.

Remember, at this point, I still didn't know I was dealing with someone with narcissistic personality disorder. I was just bored of still having to tolerate this Oscarprick around me and my business, causing havoc and disruption. And worst of all, the majority of the others were oblivious to what, or who, the root cause of every conflicting issue that presented itself had stemmed from in the first place.

I've always been divinely led. Receiving channelled information and instructions through meditating and connecting with the Most-High for guidance, is my standard practice. My guidance was to surrender any worries and follow the path I was on, and that was set for me, until the end. It would've been rude of me to tell my story and not have a happy ending to tell you right? Though more importantly, it would have been rude and disrespectful to the guidance and signs I was constantly receiving that pushed me to keep going forward, saying it's not time yet.

There were some fun moments during the filming. Like when we were shooting the playful scenes of fun and games with a cold-water hose pipe. I hate the cold. Though once I was running about fused with the warm weather it wasn't that bad. Until the sprinkle shots.

Picture this. It's starting to get cooler and the director wants me to stand around in shorts between takes of water sprinkling just behind me. It's cold. I hate the cold. And Oscar knows I hate the cold. The director gave specific instructions that nobody should talk during filming and gave direction for us two actors to follow.

During filming, Oscar is shouting out opposing instructions from the directors, saying "wet Zed up, wet him up", which made the female lead follow the instructions she could only hear, making me get wetter and colder by the second, which was pissing me off. I'm trying to remain composed, but after multiple times of Oscar repeatedly doing it, going against the directors' instructions, knowing it will piss me off, hence trying to force a reaction out of me while laughing at my frustrations, disguised as 'just being merry' to the on-looking crew, I exploded with an expletive that stunned everybody for a second. I took the following three seconds to compose myself, and continued the shoot as normal.

So what started as a fun process got rudely Oscarprickized by the covert games to break me mentally. This was during a time that was supposed to be about good productive energy, instead, the situation was used to make me look like the bad guy with behavioural issues.

It sounds childish as I'm writing, but that's the point of the game. To make you look a certain way in the eyes of others for their own amusement or so they can say "See, remember what I told you about him the other day etc..". These are just some of the manipulative strategies used to control an outcome, for whatever wonky narrative was going on in that brain of Oscars, for his own gain.

Sound familiar? The last time I encountered this level of foolishness, before Oscar, I was in a Peckham primary school around the age of six or younger. Dickhead.

Anyway, after all the screaming and women storming off set, and me somehow being blamed for that because I didn't stand up for Oscar (I'm bussing up with laughter right now), we managed to complete the weekend shoot by the hairs of our chinny chin chins, despite any disruption from the weather or anything else.

This is the point I said I was done. Witnessing the actor's level of rage and frustration from the Oscarprickarious attitudes and conduct received from Oscar, after knowing him for less than two weeks, showed me everything that I was experiencing for almost two years! It was like a wet fish slap in the face that echoed from Bristol to Pluto clearly giving me a message from the universe that was interpreted as:

"Look at what challenges you've endured and handled with grace for the past two years my divine being. Well done my warrior king Regal. You've passed our divinely orchestrated test with flying colours. Thankyou. It's time to prepare for closure. Though stay vigilant, it's not over yet"

As I'm writing this now, I'm still waiting for the videos to be completed, months after the event has passed. This is solely down to Oscar playing silly buggers', preoccupying himself with power and control games, instead of communicating adequately, with everyone necessary, to get the job complete as any manager worth the title should be capable of doing, as standard.

CHAPTER EIGHT
THE OSCARPRICK CHECKLIST

*"Protect your business, mind
and your energy."*

I N NO PARTICULAR ORDER OF IMPORTANCE, LET ME SHARE WITH YOU
a few final things I've experienced and learned, that will help
you better identify an Oscarprick in your business or life, otherwise known as an extremely toxic person.

- *Very Critical*
  Always trying to make you feel small, or wrong. Very
  judgemental of everything you do and anyone around you.
  Emotional programming is in play

- *Pathological Liar*
  He's got no integrity. You request something to be done and
  they conveniently forget, or you have to keep nagging them

to complete tasks. A need for power and control by getting you to react to their Oscarprickisms.

- **Persuasive and Charming**
  They've got the gift of the gab at first appearance. They have an overly nice and helpful public persona, but privately they're a nightmare.

- **Passive Aggressive**
  Sarcasm - Saying something positive but with an underlying negative or critical tone. Silent treatment. Subtle Sabotage - Intentionally causing small problems to undermine your efforts.

- **Lack of Empathy**
  An inability to understand and share the feelings of someone else. often seen as those with a cold response to the suffering of others.

- **Playing the Victim**
  Poor me. Life isn't fair. Oscar might always try to blame a health issue on everything, looking for sympathy. Don't fall into the trap. Give none.

- **Project and reflect**
  Nothing is ever their fault, it's always someone else's fault. They never hold themselves accountable or take responsibility for their actions.

- **Manipulation through guilt**
  I did this for you so that entitles me to....

- **Trash Talk**
  Always talking bad about other people behind their backs.

If they do it with you, they're definitely doing it about you with others.

- *Need to be centre of attention*
Look at me - Look at how brilliant, entertaining or helpful I am bollocks. Always finds themselves in the centre of a crisis or situation.

- *Boundaries*
They ain't got none. Doesn't seem to know when something is too much – like ringing off your phone twenty times at 16:01 because you said you'd be available at 16:00 type Oscarprickisms.

- *Gaslighting*
When a person manipulates another into questioning their own reality, perceptions or sanity.

And here's a few things you can do to keep yourself in check when dealing with a toxic person.

- *Your Mindset Matters* – Keep it true to yourself and your inner knowing's and beliefs. Try to limit their access to your head.

- *Don't give up*

- *Keep your emotions in check* – Any positive or negative response from you, is an opportunity to get their foot further in the door of getting in your head.

- *Don't give up*

- ***Expect them to be themselves*** – When you understand their patterns of behaviour, you are prepared and can better manoeuvre around their Oscarprickisms to achieve your desired outcome in any given situation.

- ***Don't give up***

You've got this. You are more than capable of overcoming any Oscarpade thrown in your direction.

CHAPTER NINE
THE EXIT STRATEGY

"Everything sounded like the theme tune from a Rocky film when training in preparation to win a fight."

THE ONSLAUGHT OF OSCARPRICKARIOUSNESS TOOK A TURN FOR the worst at the beginning of our second year together. Almost immediately after him saying that he was going to go back to the old Oscar. I thought to myself, "so who the flying fallopian tubes have I been dealing with all this time if you're about to introduce another side to your already messed up character."

I'd probably been recording every phone conversation with Oscar for a while, before I got to the point of saying aloud to the universe, that I was done. This was for my own protection, and proof of his words and actions, should I need them.

Combining the mental 'red flag' notes I'd been taking since the start of our relationship, and his consistent Oscarprickarious behaviour, which continued right up until the very last correspondence, I had more than enough ammunition to expose him, and his actions towards me and my business.

I could visualise his unsuspecting business partner and colleagues cracking a sticking Oscarfart in disappointment and disbelief at learning the truth, as I delivered my final words, and take my exit.

I wanted to have the meeting in person, but my back started playing up again (It's weird how the only time it ever played up in this way, was when I had to physically go and see Oscar! Hmmm...), so I wrote a detailed email and sent it to Oscar, his business partner, and bcc'd any other relevant people so that he couldn't attempt any further Oscarprickarious communications with anyone, as I anticipated he'd do, trying to wriggle out of his self-imposed rat in a corner predicament.

It was three months between the weekend video shoot and me sending the email. Though within that time, Oscar would continuously lose his composure and increase his abusive, and attempted manipulation onslaught by any means possible. I later learned that the increased panicky attempts to regain control, is a common narcissistic behaviour pattern, which Oscar tried to use to regain control of a situation he was clearly out of his depth with.

I starved him of personal contact and kept my digital communications with him to a minimum. I'd call him out on any Oscarprickisms in a calm and authoritative manner, and watch him stutter and spout more lies as a way to fill the silence I'd give him to talk, instead of responding to his nonsense. I'd continually repeat the same few business-related questions I'd asked him multiple times, knowing full well that it would piss him off and trigger him to do the exact opposite. Not answering me, or giving me the silent treatment. That was his strategy to regaining control.

He'd say dumb things that would highlight his scheming thought process and show me how on edge he had become, from no longer having as much access to me. Things like - "You're not going to sign the contract, are you?"- to which I'd honestly reply "I said I'd give you two years." Not giving a straight answer, or at least the one I knew he wanted to hear, concerning the crucial bits of information he was itching to know before making a decision on his next move, was a game Oscar loved to play.

Because I understood myself, and his patterns of behaviour, his actions only served as tool for him to cut his own throat on the run up to our final conversation. I successfully used reverse psychology on him as a means to distract him from the timing of the inevitable outcome, while being amused at his Oscarprickarious attempts to remain calm under the pressure of feeling like he was losing even more control of the power games he'd instigated.

I'd told him from the very beginning of our relationship that I am well versed at playing games, because I could see the signs and the red flags, and that I chose not to use them as a teenager because truth and honesty reign over everything. You only end up looking like a foolish Oscarprick when lies are exposed. So why bother in the first place is my mindset.

Anyway, in this final letter I highlighted several, provable points, that anyone in their right mind could see and feel was facts. They could even look into it themselves if they wanted to dig further.

But to how it was eloquently worded, I anticipated the usual, and very welcomed, no response.

As well as dropping a few YouTube links in the email that described, better than I could articulate, the dynamics between me and Oscar, I also highlighted about eight lack of professional conduct points to reinforce what was happening with absolute clarity. Here's one from that said email:

- **Professional and personal conduct in other people's homes** – You have been banned from entering a collaborative partners premises for over several months now, because of your talk and conduct with their underage daughter!

There was also a scenario where Oscar attempted to steal forty pounds off of me from an outstanding performance fee that he had arranged to be paid to him. He planned to take his agreed managers percentage off of the remaining fee and give me the rest. During my conversation with the event organiser, where I informed her of me sacking Oscar, she sent me the screen shot of the messages sent between her and Oscar confirming the actual agreed fee! This fool really did try to rob me of forty pounds!

There are so many more unwritten scenarios I could detail about my version of Oscarprick, though that would be a waste of my time and energy because I'm sure you get the drift by now.

One of the closing paragraphs from my concluding email read as follows:

"I am grateful and thankful for everything that has been realised and achieved in our time together. It has been a truly enlightening, awakening and empowering experience for me. It has become part of my life's story and purpose as a messenger, healer and lightworker to inspire and empower others creatively through the lessons, and blessings of my lived experiences."

It has been blissfully peaceful ever since the day I pressed send on that email. The worst is now behind me.

There are lots of big things currently in motion concerning my music and creative aspirations too. Though the next part of my adventure, has no room for any form of Oscarprickariousness from any form of Oscar Oscarpricks. I Am Ready.

CHAPTER TEN
EVERYTHING HAPPENS FOR ME NOT TO ME

"Your mindset is the key to everything"

ETTING RID OF AN OSCARPRICK IS LIKE, WEENING A BABY WITH teeth away from breast feeding. Slowly, the discomfort of your sore nipples from the constant nibbles become less, or, the constant crying to get the titties back becomes less. The more you show the child that all of their attempts to manipulate you emotionally, to get what they want won't work anymore, the quicker their behaviour pattern changes. The breasts might leak for a little while afterwards, meaning that there may be the occasional attempts to test their powers of past manipulations, though eventually it stops. Meaning Oscar, and the after effects of Oscar, have been fully detached and healed.

Ironically, most Oscars are a result of early life traumas. What we experience is their low self-esteemed actions to help fill that gap, through learned and mastered attack and defence mechanisms they've created over time, to protect their emotions from being hurt. And we all know that, hurt people hurt people. As with anything, positive or negative, the more you do something, the better you get at it. It's called self-programming. The key to their healing, is for them to look within and heal themselves. Though, their lack of empathy and true understanding of how to express emotions will quickly become their challenge. So good luck with that Oscar.

It's because of my life lessons from dealing with abusive personalities, personal traumas and self-healing, that I've reached a place of full understanding of myself. Some people never achieve this stage. Mainly because they're unwilling to surrender to the essential, mindset transformations that the little voice in our head often prompts us to take, but get ignored in fear of it affecting their status quo in some sense, to truly evolve in to the best version of themselves. The best version of the person we are created to be.

We all have a choice. Sometimes the hardest choice is where you find your personal truth. Personal truth can seemingly shatter your whole existence, making it feel impossible to take the seemingly mammoth task to transformation. This is why some people choose to remain in their life's bubble, repeating old and outdated patterns and cycles, while screaming to the world about being happy with life.

If you ask them what their dream life is, it's often nothing like the one they are living. I've always said, "If you want change, YOU have to be the change", which isn't easy when pride, social perception and fear get in the way of true mental, emotional and spiritual healing, which can lead to the life of our dreams.

The Super Empath and Healer side of me understands the deep challenges that Oscar is plagued with, and what he needs to do to stop being a dickhead, but now, I'm just grateful for the experience and glad to see the back of him.

If you were to sit down and think, or have a conversation, about all of the valuable life lessons you've acquired from birth, and how at every step, you were being prepared for the next part of your life's journey, it would be difficult to remember everything with clarity.

For me, this experience has been that awakening conversation.

Every time Oscar tried to be an Oscarprick, because I could see what was happening and was committed to seeing my journey through to the end, he only served as a self-reflective tool that shone light on everything I'd ever endured, overcome, and had already become a master of, like managing energy efficiently and effectively.

Instinctively actioning my wisdom in various ways to protect myself, while still moving forward in my business with Oscar, felt like it was a final test to see if I'd truly learned my life's lessons, and how I'd handle it. It felt like a real-time process of self-evaluation and understanding, before ascending to the next chapter of my life.

I'm truly in a place of gratitude and forgiveness, because in my experience, forgiveness frees ourselves from the mindsets that keep us stuck. The main purpose of forgiveness, is for ourselves. It's one of the keys to true freedom.

I've had so much fun documenting my journey that I'm a little amazed that it's taken seven days to complete the writing. If muscular issues in my back had not randomly decided to play the "you ain't moving for a week, and I'm not going to provide you with a massage therapist to help fix you" game with me, it's possible I wouldn't have had the time to write it so quickly. We all have the same 24 hours, and I've always opted to be as creative and resourceful as possible with my time. This comes from hearing I'd be wheelchair bound as a youth. It motivated me to adopt a mindset of making the most of my T.I.M.E.

Writing this book has reinforced my personal healing journey in many ways. For example, it's brought me a deeper understanding of the strained relationship dynamics between my parents and its ripple effect, along with assisting my process of closure from Oscar. Hopefully my story can offer you some valuable insights, and useful tools that you can adopt into your life, to bring closure on whatever Oscarprickisms you're faced with.

Humour can be a powerful tool to help take the edge off when things seem tough. Though if you find yourself having to deal with your version of Oscar Oscarprick, then remember, it's because you are strong, and you are someone special or of importance, why the narcissist is attracted to you. Oscar wants your power. Instead, use your power to empower yourself.

My experience and understanding of people with narcissistic personality disorder (NPD) is that, anyone can fall prey to an Oscarprick.

The key is to maintain strength of mind, have faith in your abilities, and embrace leaning on your star qualities and attributes for your highest good.

#Skidanglebom